Ending the War on My Body

Poems

Katherine McClintic

Printed in the United States of America

ISBN: 978-1-956019-48-3 (paperback)
ISBN: 978-1-956019-49-0 (ebook)

**Canoe Tree
Press**

4697 Main Street
Manchester Center, VT 05255

Canoe Tree Press is a division of DartFrog Books

Dedicated to my foremothers,
Dianne Reynolds-McClintic,
Joan Bishop-Reynolds,
Shirley Klumpp-McClintic

This book wouldn't exist without your brave steps toward
unconventional lives.

Contents

Unrest

I remember liking my clothes
and making bold choices
I suited up in what suited me

I felt like an icon, a tween idol
Hot pink capris
Lime green tank
Zebra-striped accessories

Pigtails and a too-big smile
Unplucked eyebrows
Glitter for miles.

I floated above.

Like a pin to a balloon
I remember the day
when I learned
that I didn't know
how to pretty

No one told me
But there was a skeptical squint
A snicker as I walked
Someone's mother said
"Well aren't you brave
to be so much"

My bubble popped

Though I had been me, wholeheartedly.

It wasn't pretty
Was it?

I didn't know how to pretty
so I looked
In *Cosmo*
In *Vogue*
In diet articles
In the *Reader's Digest*
Telling me to count how many times
I chew each bite of food
(which I certainly started to do)

There were no pamphlets
on becoming pretty
in the school counselors'
spinning wire racks

Yet other girls
knew the secrets
I seemed to lack.
They knew how to pretty

Who had taught them?
What could I learn?

Maybe the secret
was losing the stripes
adding highlights,
clothes fitting just right

I put on the blues and the grays
and trained in ballet
like a cadet in boot camp.
Enlisted in learning
how to pretty myself

For the good of the many
I would die for beauty
Give anything
to be rid of my belly

The glitter on my cheeks
rotted
and turned to petroleum, shame

I think I was nine
when the war began.

A Chest Open

instead of rubber
bouncing words back

I am a chest
open just a crack

the words inside settle and rest
telling me of all I lack

the chest rattles and screams
every word an attack

I'm left bleeding from words that fester
stuck like glue to my ribs
my back

My body in a chest
open just a crack

What You Believed About Me

I spent my life eating
what you believed about me
for breakfast

sly insult cereal

Fought with your words
in my mid-morning snack

Swallowed their weight
with my L-I-T-E lunch

Cumulative years of life spent
repenting meals
for no other reason than I believed you knew the
Truth
Forgive me teacher, for I have sinned

I forwent sustenance
until past sunset
Hours of sweating and sit-ups
my penitence

Nightly, by my wilting dinner
I lost control
and ate
my weight
in pasta and popcorn

Carrying that guilt of my gut,
I went to bed and knew
the same was planned
on tomorrow's menu

I spent my life eating
what you believed
about me for breakfast

My Tongue

I remember when the abilities of my tongue unfolded before me

I asked for sustenance
and received

Politely exchanged
Pleases for water

My tongue
learned
grew
expanded
developed vocabulary

The length of it strengthened
unfolded from my mind
got so long
got along
charming
disarming
getting its way

Until it met the sting
of no's and denial

With a tantrum
realized its power
to change minds
break hearts
convince and lie

Biting words
lashed out
paralyzing victims
who were girls like I

My tongue, so wise
so conniving
no one opened their lips to correct mine

My tongue became venomous
pricking victim after victim
turning friend against friend

Gossiping
sneaking
again and again

Until my eyes witnessed my tongue's crimes
told my sharpened appendage
the damage it had wrought

Instead of licking the wounds
my mouth, hating itself
swallowed the whip
my tongue had become
with the poison and the shards
tasting my blood and the blood I had shed

My tongue
curled up into shame inside my belly

Like a guilty snake
said nothing aloud
said nothing not allowed
again

Its biting words
Shame, shame
suffer, suffer
stay the same
spilled like oil
infecting my brain

The Great Tyrant

Perfection decimated everything that was not itself,
and ruled an empty spotless land.

It was not good
It was not righteous
It was only clean
(whatever that word is meant to mean)

Vicious tyrant
cleaned the trees of bees,
and the stones of dust,
vaporized anything that could rot or rust,

all texture up and went
from snakes, to whales
to long rat tails,

The tyrant deemed it unclean to breathe.

Color seen as flawed,
all pigment
was scrubbed clear
and squeaked clean
(whatever that word is meant to mean)

Buckets of blood,
filled from here to the sun.
Bleached white. Completely wiped.
Not one human atom
allowed to remain.

Perfection took
what the tyrant sought,
the world was pure
the world was clean
(whatever those words are meant to mean)

(The Mirror)

There are few objects
made so female
as a mirror
round and softly curved
atop a vanity

Made incarnate
by the eyes
of a woman,
made possession
by the pressure
of others looking on

maiden obsession
          (made in obsession)

she knows
as she powders
her nose

she knows
her powers
as the gaze
he grows

that is the vanity,
the brutal curve
of femininity

She is the object
in the mirror
lusting
to be lusted for.

But

Button Up, but
let your hair down
a little.

Cover Up, but
show some skin
(just a bit).

Tight clothes
look better
on camera, but
the camera adds ten pounds.
Be a little more fit.

Surely ten pounds
more of you
is a mortal sin.

Stand Out, but
shrink to be
a little
less.

Flaunt It, but
the fabric should be
a little
more.

Look Natural, but
dye your hair
a little
lighter.

Embrace You, but
make your abs
a little
harder.

Speak Up, but
don't giggle
a little.

Own It, but
don't brag even
a bit.

Be More, but
not more of your body.

Ten pounds more
is a mortal sin.

Ten pounds more
is a female crime.

Curves are in, but
don't let it
jiggle.

I like a girl with meat
on her bones, but

That woman is too much.

I don't like girls who are too little.

no way to win
might as well fade
so I can blend in

Basic Training

I have learned
well
how to keep
small
a mother finch
hiding her nest

fitting in the quiet nooks
and slipping through the crannies
brown as sand

cozy enough to sit
upon
invisible enough to slip by unnoticed, hopefully

You know, I won't fight
that would take up all my might
and I still may lose
risk leaving with a bruise

It seems
with each passing
year
day
I evolve to blend
my makeup
my cowardly clothes
the tone of my voice

Like she-peacocks
being beige
will keep us safe
help us secure
a protecting mate

Continuously
told to be so thin
to be small enough to fit in
your cupped hands like a
door-mouse
or do I mean -mat?
shrinking so I could be snapped
at your hands,
as if
I haven't already been.

Carnage

I'm your biggest fan.

Take my hair
pluck every last lash
String it
along my spine,
Split my phalanges to make the frets
Hollow out my hip bones
and make me a guitar
so I can be a beautiful song
you strum your fingers along

Take my skin
tan it and stretch it taut
With my femurs
and forearms
stretch my skin around my ribcage
Borrow my tibias
to drum up a beat
let all the fans and fanatics tap their feet
Gather round where my heart did pound

Break the joints
away from my shins
and whatever remains
fasten to my skull
Your lips to my jaw
make a bone-a-fide cornet
My eye sockets and nose make room for the wind
blow softly or loudly or with pursed lips
Finally
I'll be all your hopes and dreams
I'll be the band
and your biggest fan.

Tumbleweeds

I've the will of a wisp
the backbone of a bug

don't you wish
there were more here
to hold onto

desirable land
to put your flag into

but I've nothing
but tumbleweeds
and a fear of commitment

there's ghosts in this town that will give you a stiff one

so if you wish
there was more of me
to hold onto
to hold you

I suggest you move
to the plot up the road

I've heard there is fertile soil
something on the stove to boil
a strong prairie woman
with a will of steel
who can stand up tall
Someone uncrushable

Don't Cut Your Hair

hair bobbed off
equal to
losing ten pounds

feeling weightless
brand: new you!
fresh locks
give it ten weeks off
until you're missing
the power and sway
the flipping your hair
as men look your way
give it a year
until you're missing
wind in your hair
hissing
running wild
like a child

you'll shake
whinny and stamp
and grow

grow your mane back.

Between Men's Hands

Traded in corsets
for cocktails
and I don't feel very
liberated
merely libated
cuz the cocktails keep us thin.

And men still want
their fingertips to touch
while trapping our waists between their palms.

The advantage is now
we can speak
but we're too drunk
to remember the words.

Too underfed and frail
to escape the hands
clutching at our waist.

Though we are wild,

Kept so thin
We're easy to break.

Fixer-Upper

I see you across the bar
with some spackle and a spatula

"have you used that before?"
you say "sure"

Well won't you come over
because I'm a home
not quite intact.

Ain't it charming
how I need you to fill in the gaps?
Isn't it disarming
the parts of me, so delicate
they crumble into chalk?

How are you with Kaulk?

Varnish me
Harden your hat
Ramshackle me
so you can renovate
Tell me
what it is I am.

All I'm asking is for you to fill in the severed parts
to plug up and plumb the holes in the dam
of my leaking parts
and if your hand is the only thing holding
up the fragile frame, so be it.

It feels good while you're drilling.
It feels good the good you think you're doing.

Once you've lacquered me well
I'll put a ring around your left wrist
and make you feel like this house is thoroughly
flipped

We'll seal the deal
with a big to-do
I do, you do

We do too.
Then you'll move in.

Proud of this shell you've redesigned.

If the mirrors you wish to hang
don't need anchoring mounts
I'll agree

but I know it's drywall
and after a while the illusion will shatter

the walls will crumble again.

Day after day
I'll bat my lashes
as you finally open your eyes.

Isn't it darling
that I'm not independent
as advertised
Don't you think it's lovely
the needing of you that comes out of my pores

How are you with chores?

Paint Me by Number

Paint me in
scoop out all the fat and filling
and color in my skin
this pale canvas
is uninspiring
it is certainly uninviting

Paint me
by number
Color all the lines
Make me what you want of me

Let me entertain
your notions
Sell me all your pretty
potions

Just let me choose
the motions
(It's the only color I have left)

Affianced

Being wanted,
Pursued
Didn't empower me
Though at the first powerful kiss
consumed, I thought it would.

I still have all the same dreams
and all the same demons

I don't believe when you say
you love my body
as it is today

How could you when
I am seeing how soon
I can nip and tuck
and permanently pluck
all of me that grows

Being
Chosen
Deemed *the one*
Didn't make me believe I was beautiful
though the preacher said it would
Fleetingly felt gorgeous as you pulled out a ring

I still have my same bones
and all my same bruises

I don't believe you
when you say
you love my body
again today

How could you love
something so hollow
So human
So overly sized
So ugly

Rotten
inside and out
Dorian Gray in a wedding gown.

Being
Married
and Beloved
Didn't fill me up
Though I dreamt it would
As "I love you's"
"I do's"
were whispered in moon-drenched rooms

I did everything right for men
for them
and I still hate me.

I hear you say you love me as I am.
You love who I'll become.

Too bad it was me I was running from all along.

Eradicate

Magnifying glass
to my cheeks
Chin, corrupted skin

I find every misplaced hair
that light can find
and pluck it from my face

I keep searching
all the dots, spots
and freckles
that I can violently excavate
and eradicate

when my face is done
I dig up the backs of my legs
trying to find the satisfying fossils
in my follicles

and when I've poked and prodded
Drawn Blood
I fill in all the extra gaps
with products and potions
to embalm what's left

but there is always more fault to find
more Flaws to unearth
to be discovered,
defined

more
Nitpicking
one pore at a time

Prisoner of War

shell soft as skin
susceptible to every scratch
mind in a skull
that can easily crack
head's so full of contradictions
it may do just that

legs that move
me around the world
why have you betrayed me
with the size of your
gelatinous thighs

hands that are burdened
with striving texting reaching
why have you betrayed me
how can I use hands this
witchy and huge?

et tu boo-tay?
a knife to the lower back
why have you betrayed me
who would give you so much as a pat,
fallen flat?

I'll whisper to my belly fat
"we were never friends,
like that"
you've never been quite right
always pinchable
never tight
you have betrayed
every single oath
since you were never
as I hoped

here I stand
Prisoner of War
should I sit,
capitulate?

must I accept the borders
the boundaries
of me and this damn skin
it's everywhere
I am in

Fighting

Seal my esophagus
I'm not eating anything
I won't give into hunger
the illusion of need
I shouldn't eat past five

So I'll have coffee
instead of a meal
asparagus alone
is all I need to dance all day
and party all night
I won't eat that block of cheese
when I get home tonight

I won't finish my plate
I'll look dainty
and faint

No, I won't go eat.

Tape my eyelids open
I'm not missing anything
I won't retreat into sleep
into this illusion of need
I don't want to miss my life

So I'll fight off sleep
with my fists
and I'll burn up all the pixie dust
and I'll shear all
the counted sheep

No, I won't go to sleep.

Trenches

What am I avoiding
and burying deep
down
where dreams fade
and ideas fail
to come to term?

at least you are the same
as you were before
in this new comfortable place

surely I've done
all the growing
leaping
failing
and weeping
and gnashing of teeth
as my expectations of
my reflection
and distributed persona
reach new heights
of insurmountability

best to go around the mountain
better on the joints
the bones
the ego bruises

but maybe the crying
and climbing
and slipping
and gripping
and sweating
and bleeding
are actually all
what victory looks like
atop something insurmountable
carried by your hands and legs
your insignificant limbs stretching
at the peak of a mountaintop

What image is more triumphant

or more terrifying?
a slip and a tumble from plummeting to your death

everything feels safer at base level
the site of the expectations I'm not climbing
lead me to a lifelong
chore
of digging
my dreams and ideas
my reflection
and persona
deep down
in a hole

I'm down here, trying to hide
Will I simply die here at the base of a mountain
my ideas like jewels in a casket
buried,
as if getting old is enough to show for a life?

What am I avoiding and burying deep down?
Do I want to be the same as I was before?

What is more frightening,
the shovel or the summit?

Squeaky Wheel

grease my joints
hear the early creaks
that aging wreaks

Wince, oh my back
a catch in the knee, grimace

I'm not rotting yet
try not to forget

scrub off the rust
see the early hues
neglect and misuse

Popped ankles,
heart stopped from a trip
hope I don't need new hips

not rotting yet
try not to forget

not crumbling away
at least not today

Hairs, skin
all out of place
Is this my face?

not rotting yet
tell myself not to forget

getting older's your whole damn life.

the body may weaken
the skin may sag
the eyes may dim

But I've not done my soul in?
There's always time to begin?

grease my joints
hear the early creaks
that aging wreaks

Gr8ful

the truth is I am fine
I've got everything I need
and love as far
as the human eye can see

the truth is my life is full
it's bursting
but my glass
always runs out
because I am thirsty

and I'm left
feeling very human
very small
a lonely goldfish
the universe a waterless bowl

it appears I'm doing great
but, I'm never full

Treason

I'm sure I'm fine.
but there's thoughts in my head
so toxic
my stomach must digest them
so slick and syrupy
my lungs feel full
so fearful
my heart runs away

But I'm sure I'm fine.
I know words like *psychosomatic*
and *pseudo*
I know about phantom pains
and aches
but it feels so real

I'm sure I'm fine.
it just smells like filth and rot
bodies and puke
Or am I imagining all the smells
that make me sick too?

I'm sure I'm fine.
except for the bugs
gnawing on my skin
Now I am sure of it.
I can feel the bites
itch
the ants
or worse.

Crawling up my arms.
Colonizing my neck.
They're so real
I'll have to pack all my belongings into plastic bags
I'll be as good as a leper
in this city
plagued by bugs.

A thorough inspection
a magnifying glass
no bugs.

I think I'm fine.

If I think therefore I am fine
and you are what you eat
I am nauseous because I think I am
I have become spoiled
by my lunch. It definitely was sketchy
Wasn't it?
My brain can't
forge everything, that's philosophy gone too far.
My body is sick
is betraying *me*, this is not my mind.

This is real. I'm fine.

the poison food
must come up
the knot tightens
a sudden exit from the conference room

everyone at the office ate the same thing

Why am I the only one with knees on checked linoleum
coughing, hair pulled back?
What comes out is real.

Was that the fourth time this week?

I'm not sure I'm fine.

Shrapnel

Flowers and praise being thrown my way
I don't feel any of the warmth.
Why don't I feel applauded?
Why aren't kind words good enough?

I stretch out clutching
for soothing words that have been said
searching in my medicine cabinet for praise that gave me permission to be,
but I come up grasping the daggers
and the dirty looks instead.

The sharper the word, the better.
The more it gets in, festers
begins a life of its own.

Why does catching a compliment feel so dull
Never breaking skin, not even able to make a cut, paper thin
when I've had to hand-stitch
flaps of bleeding tissue
torn from the cutting words.

No soft word was ever more
than a placebo

And I'm looking for the penicillin
the one word
the one dose of approval
to cut inflammation.

What doctor will magically heal
the gaps,
the stitches and scars,
scalpel off the bitter words growing on my heart?

Who can heal me
from all the words that have been biting and harsh?

Numb

Waking up next to you
I still wake in my body

Same toes
Same nose
Same clothes I chose

Same mind
Same soul
Same heart you stole

And all I want is change
And forward motion
Where are we going,
I've got no notion

Waking up one with you
Still it's my body

And all I want is to be other
Waiting for perfection
Where is old Godot?
Maybe if I try a new confection

A pinch of this
A dash of that
Collecting all the little bits
of all those more beautiful people

Mix them all together and be
new new new and improved

But I wake up
and it's still my body

Same nose
Same toes
Same closet of clothes

Same lips
Same hips
Same shin splints and bones

When will waking up this way
feel a little more peaceful
a little more okay?

Tomb of the Unknown Soldier

I am a tombstone
date of birth
slash
year of death
a million
little identities
lived
in between

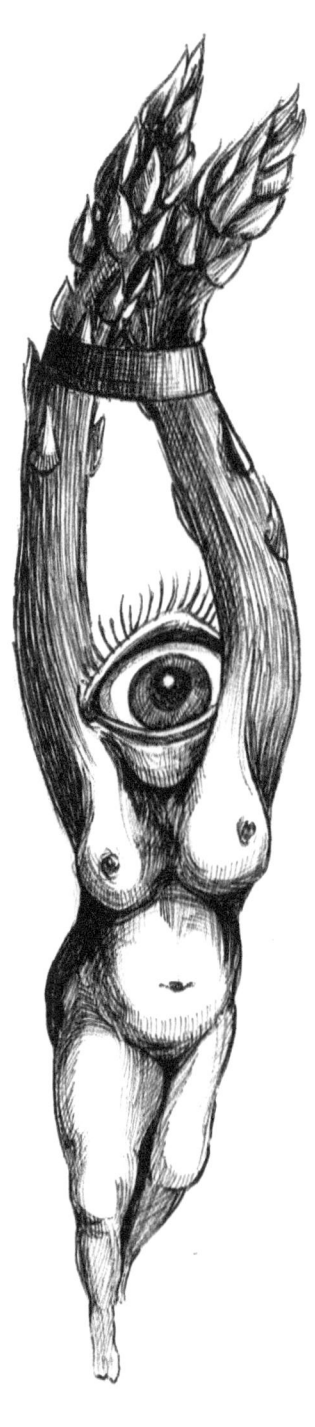

Taking My Body to Market

My mind expanded
upon realizing

that all the people
living in the bodies
I would have happily exchanged
for my own
(even if just
for store credit)

were shells for souls
just as willing
to put a price
on the way their flesh hangs
on the way their bones grow
on the way their muscles
reflect the seeds they sow

the way they are wrong.

That the bodies I wanted
all wanted to change
if not their stomach
then their cheeks
and their nose.

We have all been drafted
crafted
to hate the bodies we live in
no matter how thin

or desirable
or thick
or broken.

What if we were all worthy
of growing the way we grow,
gaining the way we gain,
beautiful as humans
not as prizes
to be gained?

Maybe it's time to believe
the lovers who have lavished
in my softness
and reveled at my sharp tongue
who held enthusiastically
to the thighs
that thundered
(which I confused for weakness)

Maybe I will allow
my body to grow
as it grows
and water
and feed it
to facilitate
my soul.

Maybe life's worth living in this body
after all.

Horror Film

Don't go there, girl.
Don't go into the depths
that long for you.

The rock-bottom places
that taunt you to return
with their sickly siren songs
It's a lie that perfect beauty was possible all along

Steer the boat the other way
Don't go there, girl
Not today.

I am not required
to hate my curves and thighs

I was not designed
to regret my own face

I cannot be made
to count all that I eat and all that I expend
like a Stepford machine
designed for men.

Don't go there, girl.
Don't be pulled under
by creatures with their tarred,
webbed hands
showing you the way
through shadowed haunted caves

You've already been at the bottom of the sea,
Starving,
wondering *if* you should eat.

Don't go there, girl
Not today.

Listen to your body
it's the audience
that is watching you
like a horror film
Don't open the door.
Don't open the door!

You don't have to go there, girl,
leave that knob locked.
You know what is behind it lurking
There's nothing new behind that door to find

It is the nothing
The void
The shadows
The upside-down
The locked and empty room
where you'll meet your doom.

Climb out the window
Run free, the audience begs of you,
please!

Don't go there, girl,
Don't open the door.

Lack of Stillness

does my lack of stillness
make me restless
does the desire
for novelty
give me the gun to fire
at the life I chose for me?

is it so wrong to want to live

so big?

Master of None

I don't fit into the dress
I don't fit into the one-size-fits-all
I could never be small
enough,
could I?

I don't fit into these borders
I don't fit into picket fence boxes
I could never commit
enough,
could I?

Always afraid I'm lacking singular focus
Always afraid I'll miss my moment
I could never achieve a full
enough life,
could I?

I'm trying
to wring out a life
while being told to stay on a line
that is choking me.

What is it to choose one path
with such little time?

I want to do everything
be everyone
breathe every breath

I've never been okay staying on one road
when there's a scenic path to the left

I'll never be enough of any one
always Master of None

Maybe it's enough to be
Mistress of Me

Restless Joy

I have a joy that fidgets
I have a joy
that grows frequently hungry
the dandelion
thirsty for water
wrapping speedily around the roots
of sterile astroturf
One patch of land, scraps of sky
and driblets of rain not enough for her wild
She must seed wishes,
move elsewhere.

(they call the dandelion a weed)

I have a joy
who fidgets
like a curious child in her seat
beginning with the itch of the knee
then a roll of the ankle
a dramatic lean forward
head
on hands
on knees
back again.
Pulling
at the fringes of skirt
then hair
the tapping of toes
the rhythm of joy
ready to share.

only standing, twirling
on seats and pews
will seem to do—

(until it is all too much. They say
Sit still, behave)

I have a joy
who can't put her feet up

everybody loves it
this dancing joy
wanting to bottle it up
these big smiles
kinetic wiles

(but it's too much, the wrong place,
read the room, inconvenient time,
calm down, come down,
put your feet up, stay put)

I have a joy that burns
a long fuse.
It's easy to meet matches,
and logs to light
the more the merrier
and merrier she makes them
around her heart's bonfire.

(she burns too brightly.
Onlookers wet their fingers
give her a pinch)

I have a joy
That I've been told is (too hungry
too restless
too wild
too fleeting
shamefully discontent)

But I have an active joy
that blooms where it's planted
burns luminous,
frenetic.
Like a hummingbird my joy
flits always finds friends
who lend their perch on which to nest.

Through binoculars the spectators speculate
(it must be hard to be that restless bird's
branch)

Can I have a joy that breaks free of them?

Taste of Freedom

What was it like to feel free?
I can only seem to bite into it
in the moments in between
work and chains and purchased time

I know there was once a time
when I was unburdened
and I filled the space around me
with permission I've since abandoned

Am I ready to move again?

Shell Shock

eyes gaze
into the mirror
my body
so disconnected
by the haze
of years of hazing it

I don't know what I look like
anymore.

eyes zoom in on the little bits
this flaw
my crooked jaw
it's automatic
after all

and I don't remember
Was my stomach worthy enough today?

Am I allowed to ask that anyway?

eyes gaze
again
in the mirror
through the blur
lift my shirt
and find some dirt

eyes turn away
blind to my wholeness
What do I even look like?

eyes gaze
into the mirror
my body seems so disfigured
I don't know what I look like anymore

eyes gaze
at my reflection
with a breath
focus
and say the words
a modern healer
taught me to say
I'm grateful for my legs
I'm grateful for my shoulders
I'm grateful for a healthy body
Grateful to grow older.

It's Worth Living

To be a magnificent tree
you gotta get old.

Old like the willows
Old like the oaks
Old like the crones
spinning spells in their cloaks

Large trees weathered the weather.
Those trees with their countless rings
who survived fire,
face-lifts and fad diets
are the ones who get to their highest height yet.

You've gotta get old.

to be an interesting scotch
you've gotta age.

Age like the seasons
Age like the stones
Age like your grandmother
wished to have grown

Age long enough to soak up the memories and notes,
to have all the flavors
the tastes of the barrel

You've gotta age.

to go down in history
you've gotta have time

Time to be weary of living
but choosing to wake, do dishes anyway.
Time to see clearly
all the paths you thought lost.
Time to know all the "no's"
didn't amount to dying alone

Time for all of your work
for all you've learned
to look down, look back
and notice you've grown
into a valiant tree
a top-shelf bottle
a victor in battle

You've gotta have time.

You've gotta have decades to know
that the haunted dreams of your youth
held no future truth.

There's a peace to the passing years
one day you'll realize
you've survived all your deepest fears

You've gotta age, babe.

A Breath

Mirrors
Marley
and a barre

Melodies
meet you
where you are

No style needed
genre irrelevant
all you need
a body
a mind

A slight bend
of the knees

An arm overhead
a side step,
rotation
twirls

and then
your soul
shows up,
begins to mend.

(I Broke Them)

The mirrors are broken
(I broke them)
And I think it was always a lie
that breaking mirrors would bring bad luck
for seven years

Because
in my blood
there are blessings
Fortune, Abundance
(the locks of my hair are lucky charms)

I see.
No need to deform
to whatever the nameless gaze
demands beauty be.
I no longer need to see
how the pulled-apart pieces of me are perceived

The mirrors are broken
(I broke them
with sticks, with stones
with truth like a hammer)
I heard the glass sing
with the metal and bone
that struck clean.
Saw the veins and panes
splintering
and what once had held
me under its spell

was now just
shiny shards, trivial as dust

The mirrors are broken
(I broke them)
I stepped barefoot through the shattered
looking glasses
while my fists and feet bled,
a benediction

The mirrors are broken
(I broke them)
The cracking didn't break my mother's back
It exposed the fictions and fracturing
preventing my soul and spine from aligning

My body is finally invited
to the ball
with a magical choice,
instead of the vanity table's voice

The mirrors are broken
(I broke them)
My ligaments and limbs intertwine
with my hips who sway side to side.
As if for the very first time,
my Body chooses my path
one step at a time.

The mirrors are broken,
I broke them.

And I know in my soft tissue
in the marrow of my bones
in the slow-healing scars
from the infinite shards
what power is within
my rebellious, aging skin

The mirrors are broken
I broke them!

Reflection

glimmers on the water
simmering thoughts
through waves
instead of mirrors

mind tousled
and unrelenting
eroding the resolve
to appear fresh and clean
and new new new

(maybe this isn't resolve
eroding
but the freedom to, at last,
evolve)

reflections in the water
ruminating sans mirror
glass shatters
as the ocean meets me
opens my eyes to the sea

cuts on cliffs
aren't perfect
not every bit is smooth
there's hardly an ounce of symmetry
those tides are of the moon

and in the cliff's
scars and blemishes,
pools of life
abloom

if the scars of rocks
can cause such life
think of what
a broken brain
can do.

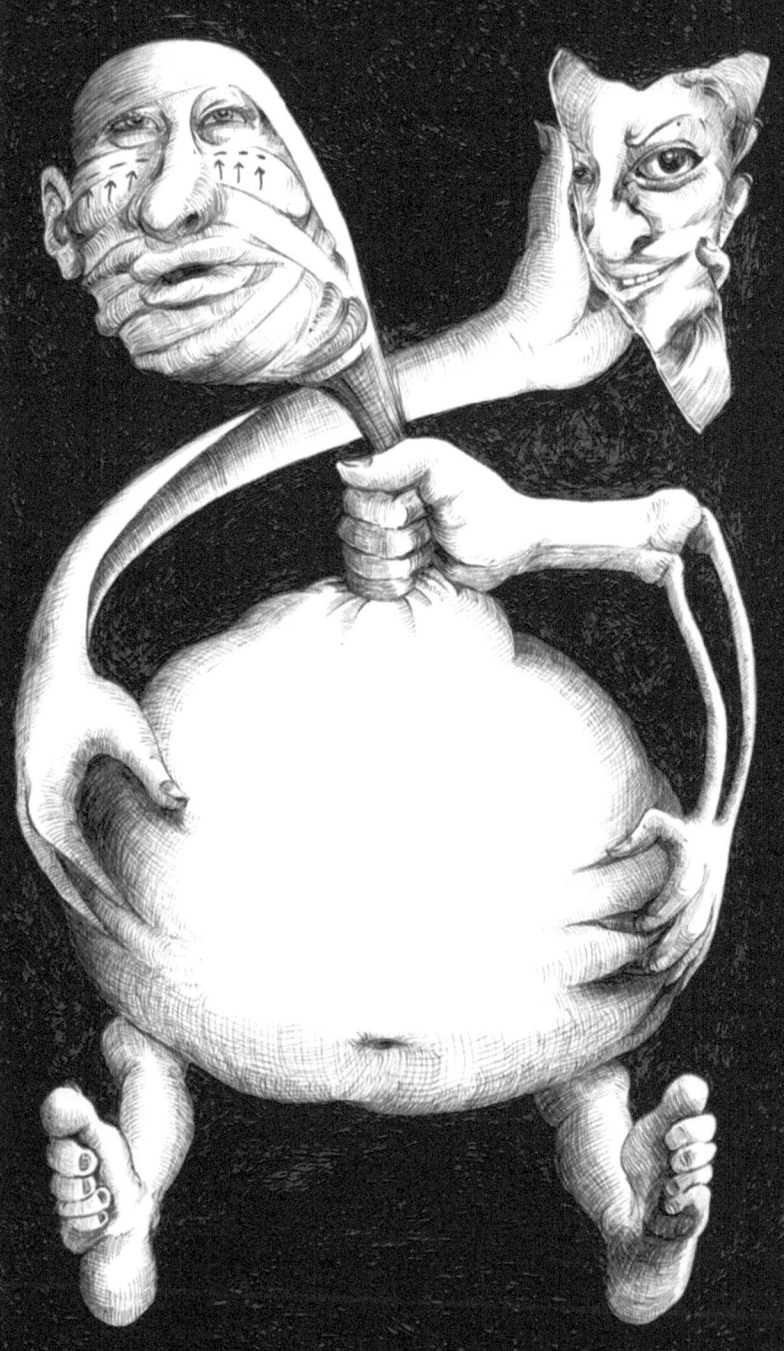

Ending the War on My Body

I am ending the war on my Body
I am ending
the war waged
on my abdomen
the battles fought
with my inner thighs

I am walking
away from the propaganda
slandering my well-concealed ribs
covering my ears
from the shell shock of lies

I am raising
the white flag
breaking all the fun-house mirrors
surrendering to the hope
I'll be a Body I don't despise

I am signing
a peace treaty
with the shape of my face,
from the arch of my eyebrows
to my crooked teeth,
I declare this war
waged on my Body
ended.

feast now
all you victorious
women

A Toast

Pumpernickel crisped
Butter melting on toast—tastes
of joy once denied

No guilt in my belly
No shame in my sight.
Jam or marmite on sourdough
A simple (carbohydrate)—delight.

Vows & Treaties

This is my vow
to take care of thee, my Body
from this day forward

To tend to the aches
and pains
as if you were the body
of my lover

To feed the needs
and hunger pangs
as if you were the body
of my child

I will feed thee

Not just to nourish
not just to convert
calories to
glucose

But to fan the flame of pleasure
in taste, in sensation, in celebration
as if you were the body
of a treasured guest

In pleasure and in pain
satiated and hungry
in thinness and in fullness
in illness and in wellness

To nourish and to cherish

Till death when my soul departs

I will be fed
mind, Body
heart, soul

Hindsight

I'm old and longing
for the body I despised
Maybe youth isn't wasted
if it's realized

What if I'd longed for me then
like I long for her now
when I see youth
contort to fit in

Except maybe the collagen,
I don't miss anything
about my younger skin.

I don't miss
the high stakes
believing I was always
bound to break
but I was so elastic then

What good is elastic
if you don't know you'll bend?

I don't miss the heartache
even though now my bones ache,
the brutal longing
for ribs poking out,
the running scared, the spinning out

Maybe I miss the porcelain smooth skin
but I don't miss the picking and peeling
it paper thin.

There were so many roads
to travel down then
so many moments I was never in

I don't yearn
for the days
giving all of myself away
certain I was not okay

When my guts were poisoned
with the inky oil spills
of shame upon shame

Don't take me back
to the days
where I said yes, but meant no
and said no
for fear of yesses
leading to successes.

I'm old and only longing
for the people who were still breathing
for the younger me who didn't know
who she was missing

I long for her to love
her head to her toes and the blood binding it all
I long for her heart
more than I'll ever long for the body
I despised.

Permission

I am allowed to show up gently for my day.
To tenderly kiss my toes to the floor,
to flex and point before burdening them with weight.
I am allowed to piddle indeterminately.
To forgo the morning trumpets and push-ups.
I am entitled to breathe in and out
without the need or the rush to do anything else.
It is my right to relish being
an alive person.
Permission granted to show up gently for the day.

Yolk

I want to crack my life
wide open
let the yolk
weighty syrupy
spill on all the bits of shells
blown open
Let what is fertile
make a river

I want to break my life
wide open
and leave the empty shards
of bones and urns
strewn behind me
in their charred
utter
emptiness.

I want to break my life
wide open
and have the yolk
flow over everything
and saturate
me with seeds of life

so I can break those seeds
wide open
and proclaim
"New life"
and break those words
wide open
and birth hope
which broken
unfolds in the daylight
Then I'll plant all the broken bits
tend to them in the ground
of the yolk riverbed
Cultivate
Fertilize
Water and Read To
the broken pieces
of past me's
turned seeds.
And maybe
just maybe
find full growth.

Before & After

Before you had authority
teaching teens
gatekeeping dreams

After years you've traded dance
for dealing diets
living for Befores & Afters

Now you are who you were
more boldly
teaching grown men and women
what you had taught me
Too tall, work the weight off, sit-ups, stay small

So that *is* how you saw me After all.
My Body was always the Before
never rewarded even though
I tried and tried
skipped meals and lied

I was never After enough.

Your boasting Before & After photos
are damning proof
that skinny was the goal
Before & After all these years.

I want to yell
at the images
"She will hurt you"

That you're teaching without testimonials
from any of the children
you fucked up.
Tell-all
you're irresponsible
with the trust
and the dollars invested,
with the words
you fed us
for Breakfast.

Part of me is satisfied, full
that all the power you held over me Before
has become something so petty and dull.

After all, I now stand so tall
boobs out, no longer smashed down

The girl I was before wants to laugh and gloat
and say I won, I won, I won.

That fleeting sweet feeling of victory
quickly sours into pity
that shrinking yourself
coaching others how to disappear
is what you feel you must do to be seen.

As a woman I see you
and pity that your Afters
come Before
feeling worthy and whole.

Color

I want to dance like poetry
in incomplete sentences
full of meter and meaning

I want to dance like paintings
be it Kandinsky or Dalí
melting swirling lines
of music and dreams

I want to dance like birds
like bees
coming out of the places
in between
the you's and me's

I want dance dipped
in symbolism
color and metaphor

I want to dance
to be more free than I was before

I want to dance
as if more is more

A Prayer to Age

Soften me up
leave me wide open,
soft velvet
and tender
a person not happy to mope
a person determined to hope

Soften me up
with each passing year
like a good pair of jeans
or sherry
(so I hear)

Make me more plush
and huggable
make my heartstrings
more tuggable

and find me a gentle place to rest
because with age
I think softness is best

Open my heart
so sharing makes me bleed
Turn my pain
into empathy

Let my coarse hands trust
they're done
toiling through the mud
Let the soil and soul under my nails
plant, seed, and bud

Blur my eyes
with laughter and lament
Let me see the world
through them, as it's meant

Let me chuckle with mirth
rather than bitter mocking at youth
save that bitterness for my coffee
and the inevitable
sharp moments of loss

Make me pliable and open
yet content with the life
I had chosen

Keep my smile lines
well used

Let my mind expand
as my Body expires
keep me soft
as one who inspires

Peace

Softer now
a touch more plush
than I once was.
My blind devotion
to thinness
has since faded
like sweat dried on skin

Calmer now
a breath more tranquil
than I once was.
The anxiety
the fear, the hiding of tears
that now rush like a river
overcoming the dams

Recovered now
A sliver more healed
The pointed words
of irresponsible adults
that drew blood
are now the faintest of scars,
a little right of the heart

Dreamier now
a hint more magic.
My imagination
once locked up
like that stuckness of wind knocking
out of your lungs,
has been freed

Resilient now
with calloused feet
that didn't retreat.

Softer now
as an adult
a touch more plush
like at the start.

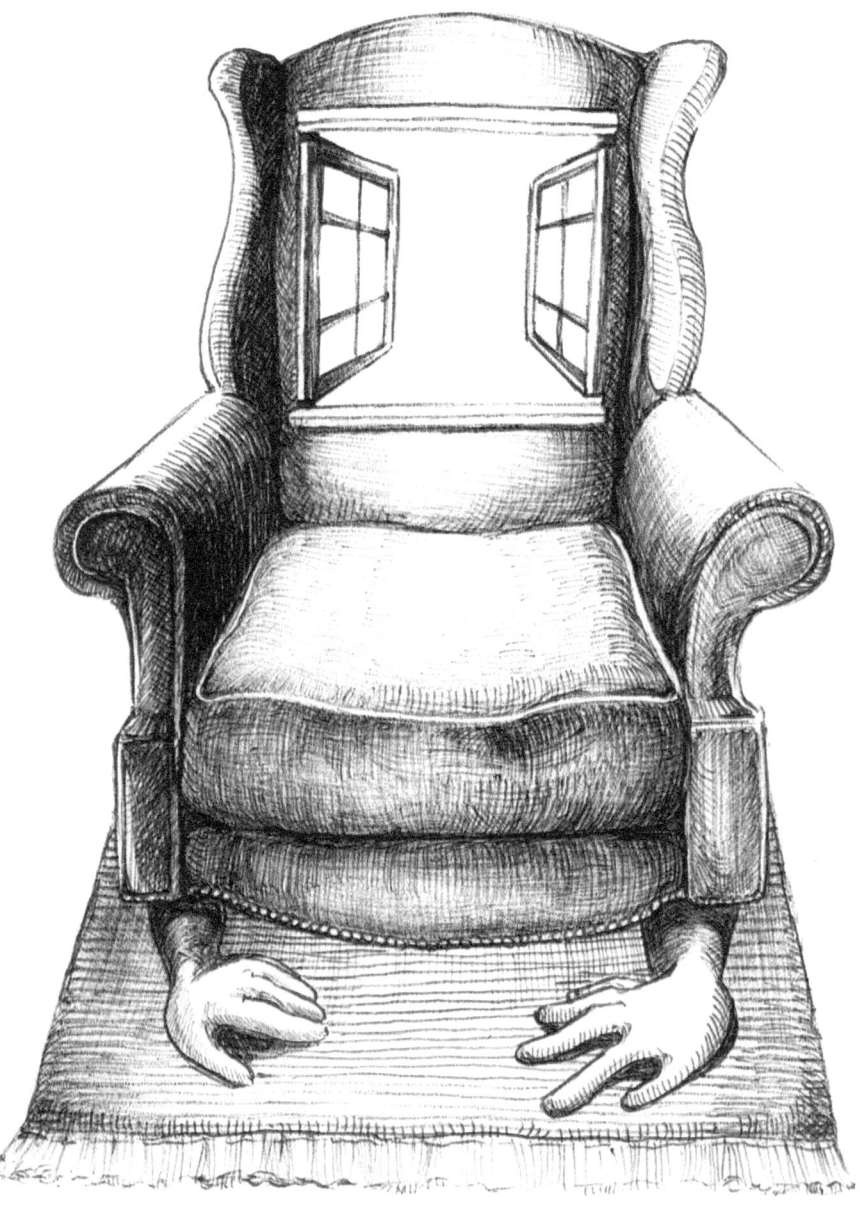

Homecoming

I healed
and no one cheered

No one cried "bully!"
No stadium waved
the white flags of surrender
while I read poetry
that had once chapped my forlorn lips

I unwrote the curses
written into my skin
by ancient warlocks

and no one came to the midnight showing.

I could breathe out
instead of always sucking-in
And no one wrote a story.
It didn't make the front page of the *Times*

(though that exhale took a long, long time)

I didn't die
on the battlefield
of Beauty

I didn't come home with a patch over my eye
not a single amputated limb.

Yet when I reflect on my journey back
I often cry.

So I wrote about it
I popped the champagne

I made it important
told everyone I was coming home
from the war of self-loathing

I stepped off that train
with my baggage and stories

And it's like I could see my mother on top of the hill, buoyant
And my father proposing a toast, jaunty
And my lover running toward me, wanting
And my friends lending their shoulders, holding

Though the presses and the hordes
weren't there that day

we threw our own parade
Declared this the national holiday
of finding solace
in our skin

in the communities we are in.

At my stadium
full of friends
you could hear the love for life

and after our fireworks
the lingering smoke
the very last joke

At the end of the war
and the party

as a victor I
finally slept

in my
Home, Body.

Is That My Body?

I emerge
wiping
the last blurs
and shards
from my eyes.

Done with a swim
I see my reflection
in the water.

Is that *my* body?

Is this lovely
stomach
the one I excommunicated?
What's wrong with softness
that curves and rounds;

it must mean my body
is related to stones
filed and caressed
by waves
rolling their way to shore.

Is that *my* body?

Are these the legs
I once fought to disguise?
What's wrong with the
sturdy-curvy of my thighs?

It just means
I'm like that tree
with sure, strong roots
thickening to uphold
its trunk and branches
knobbed
like knees.
Stump before leaves.

My eyes gaze
they're more windows
than mirrors now.

It is my body that I see
that fits in on earth so naturally

lips juicy as berries bursting
laugh singing like morning birds

nose dainty as a curious doe
toes cunning as a cougar's.

Is that my body?
Lounging like dunes
immense and peaceful
beneath life's many moons.

The mirrors are memories
I see my reflection
washed in water
and moonglow more and more.

The softness I once hated
I suddenly adore.

Revolution

It's a revolution
to like one's own eyes
thighs
scales
et al.

The battle cry,
a libretto
"I like who I am
as I am today"

What is more shattering
than her operatic high note?
Singing that libretto so shrill
she breaks
all the glass cages
she'd been put on display in.

It's a revolution

Let her eat cake!

Space

Take up space
all stars who have fallen
each particle in the threads of your skin
from the heavens above

Take up space
let your arms splay
your fingers formed
from the Milky Way

Take up space
let your life orbit
your rotating routine
another year sunlit

Take up space
and sip your tea
and watch the birds
and call your friends
all devised of stardust too

Wear Hats
Be Much
Get Fat
Find Your Fill

There's space
infinite space
ever expanding
out there

Born Again

I was born
when I began to make

I was alive
when the first breath
of an idea made it to my lungs
and I exhaled a creation

I was fetal
until I began to pump
blood and sweat
into the carvings
of my mind

My heart beat better
when I shared
her words with a lover

My soul
glowed brighter
when I reflected the lights of strangers

Could I have been my own mirror all along?

I was born
when I began to make

I was kept alive
by my ideas surviving
the dead of night.

Victory

I will hang the victories
of my life
upon the deep rolls
and wrinkles
of my aging skin.

I will hang the victories
of my life
upon the lost elasticity
from a life stretched
to the brinks of expansion
then let slack
only to be stretched again
like taffy
like the kneading of bread
like all the rubber bands
that held
my hair back
as I pummeled through life.

I will pin the victories
of my life
to my crow's feet
imprinted
by all the days and nights
smiling

The old broken records of
oh I shouldn't
and *I was going to clean*
were nothing when met
with the orchestra
of endless laughter
from infinite loved ones.
This was the music that drowned out the voices
The music I danced to, boisterous
I will hang these ballroom memories
on my hearing aids
and my fragile knees
to prove it.

Society
will have lost all desire
for me to don a crop top
and I will, defiant, chop chop all
my shirts off
just to show my ribs
and the skin
that screams
I made it through
all my hatred
and the world's abuse!

I will don the victories of my life
with my stomach hanging out
So damn proud.
Victorious
over all the viciousness.

My mind, my soul, my heart
have embraced my Body
with the love they always had.

I will sigh, speak, sing, and laugh
in my voice, growing ever feeble

"Home at last, home at last
I've made it home at last"

Afterword: Poems from High School

This book was born from my early high school poetry, where I was in denial about my disordered eating. I like to look back at it because it was written by a teen girl who knew she was okay but couldn't shake the weight of how leotards, a chaotic world, and early puberty made her feel.

It felt wrong to exclude these two early pieces from this book, so enjoy these poems that first made their appearance in secret blogs in my teen years while I cringe and pretend they are still hidden on Myspace.

Apples and Oranges Don't Compare
(April 13, 2008)

vomit on vogue—
regurgitate the lies
and pricey
images
of perfection
they shoved
down your throat

they were only illusions
alluding to
your self-esteem
and pocketbook
most likely the latter

the manufactured
plastic face
taught you to despise
true reflection

and that snapshot snuck into your soul

skinny girls
born with amazing metabolisms
or a quick gag reflex
paraded down
runways,
sang your favorite songs,
and got the perfect Ken

all the while pretending
to be the highest standard
every man's cup of tea

confused we set our standards
upon weak foundations
of sticks and little girls
which big bad wolves
always destroy

comparing moms to models
neglecting truths
of two incomparable
compositions

since when
were women
senile?
comparing peas to carrots
apples to oranges
Are you a circle or a square?
Hourglass or wristwatch-shaped?

if you feel
Orange
is the way to go
then by all means
purge

but only on vogue
they enabled you to binge
on candy-coated lies

manufactured by middle-aged men

Green Goo That Claimed It Was Good (February 11, 2009)

that's all there is
voices in my head...
I knew the smoothie
that resembled a polluted pond
wouldn't taste good,
but I bought it...
I bought a drink called Green Goodness
and the Good tasted like pond
yes, like a pond.
why? because apparently things that are green
are good for your body
they make you skinny
and perfect
and happy
and you should eat more green goodness
right?

that's all there is
these voices in my head
I know I can dance!
I have worked to perfect my plié
(though I never will)
thousands of people praised
my face, and my heart
the fun they had
while watching me twirl
I make people happy
but all it takes is one girl...
to ignore me

and look at me like goo
as if everything I ate
that didn't look like a pond
was painfully obvious
on my hips, my thighs
my stomach, my chest
telling me I should give up now
all it takes is that voice
(that never cares to say anything to me)
to make me want to give up now
and drink green goo

until she can pay attention to me
look at me like I'm healthy
a worthy contribution
like green goodness
that's actually goo

but I won't
I can't,
I can't neglect the goo
in goodness
and I want to be more than green
everyone knows that's not an easy color to be
I don't want to drown
in pond scum
and I am strong enough to dance my way out
I'm thin enough
I'm good enough
but every time she's around

I gag on the green goo
try making it taste like paradise

but that's something the juicer cannot do

Acknowledgments

We do nothing alone. We are all so brilliantly interwoven. Here are my heartfelt thanks for the threads of help I can trace, without whom this book wouldn't exist.

Dianne McClintic, my mother who read at least one book a day my whole life and taught me the joy of books. Her generosity made this book and accompanying creative projects possible. Doug McClintic, my loving father, an orator and poet in his own right. He coached me every step of the way in bringing this book to life without betraying its message and called me from different time zones in celebration whenever a landmark moment occurred. My late grandmother, Joan Bishop Reynolds, who supported my unconventional life and ultimately made this passion project possible. You're alive in everything I make.

Caleb Wiese, you ground me and take me galaxies away. No one loves me so well and leads me toward the next expansive thought like you do. Your heart and brain speak the same language, and I've learned so much from your constant willingness to abandon ideas that exclude others. Thank you for teaching me to say oops, and that so many of the small things we obsess over are morally neutral.

Thank you to my early readers who kept cheering me on. Garlen Maxson Vickers, the first to notice this pattern in my work, the first I boldly read poems with: thank you for seeing me and telling me again and again that I had something to say. Elizabeth Woods-Darby, who helped me tell the truth with great bravery and elevated each poem: thank you for being the collaborator I have searched for my whole life. My brilliant developmental editor, Elissa Sweet, who so graciously refined the structure and tension of the book as a whole while also cheering me on as my soul-sister.

Cait Jones, for her haunting, surreal, and captivating art that spoke for my poems before I could. This project was immediately expanded because of your eye, artistry, and friendship every step of the way.

My creative catalyst, Liz Kimball, who cast the vision for this book without even knowing the poems already existed. I am eternally grateful for your guidance, vision, and community, which were essential to this book and revolutionary to my life as a whole. Thank you for asking my legs for their opinion, and helping me create a contract with this project.

This book also was coaxed into existence by the other brilliant women I met through Liz Kimball's collective, especially the women who were in the "Incubator" with me during the most tumultuous year of all our lives. A special shout-out to Samantha Evans for providing extra touchstones and support throughout the process that kept me on track.

Erin Piel Bybee—my soulmate. We've made it. Thank you for being my partner in this long road of healing and for introducing me to the world of intuitive eating. Lindsey Bristol, who is one of the first people I remember admitting my struggles with body image to in a meaningful way.

Liz Beck, whose sharp wit, professional expertise, and own creative courage paved a way for me to make this book. Gillian Bell Weeks, who celebrates and commiserates like the best of them. Quanie Broadhead, for taking me to a poetry slam at Nuyorican Poets Cafe—that is the night I first dreamed of putting my poems in a book. I am grateful for her listening to that vision and for always asking the people around her to grow.

Paul Zielinski, Janice McDermott, and Deb Andre: thank you for teaching the arts and being a safe place to land when I was young in a new state.

Thank you to the team at DartFrog and Canoe Tree Press who helped all the logistics of this book come to life—Suanne Laqueur, production coordinator extraordinaire; Mark Hobbs, for all the revisions on the cover; and Taylor Graham, for proofreading the book with skill, grace, and intuition. Thank you, Gordon McClellan, for inviting me into Canoe Tree Press in a very encouraging way.

For all of the activists, HAES dieticians and nutritionists, fitness specialists, therapists, clinics, and doctors who are dispelling the myths of diet culture: thank you for the work you do to strengthen the resolve we all need to end the war on our bodies.

Special thanks to C.S.E. Cooney for being an early reader of the book in the midst of her own book launch.

To the woman I didn't know who told me she wished she had seen herself as beautiful when she was young: you opened my eyes.

Thank you, reader. You will shape this book in ways I never dreamed possible, and I can't wait to see where you take these words. If you have ended, are ending, and will end the war on your body, let's feast. The world needs you to be at peace with yourself.

About the Author

Katherine McClintic is a choreographer, poet, and the founder of the online dance community Inbox Dance Party. She moved to New York City straight after high school and now works in TV, film, and theater in NYC and LA. Katherine was a closet poet until now, and *Ending the War on My Body* is her first book. Katherine is passionate about sharing her journey to body acceptance in a visceral, imaginative way, because she previously longed for art, dance, conversations, and music in her own healing journey to supplement therapy and medical resources. *Ending the War on My Body* is in production to become a multimedia performance event combining Katherine's choreography and poetry through film, dance, music, and visual art in collaboration with many amazing artists.

Learn more at www.katherinemcclintic.com.

.